HOW TO WRITE
PERFECT
PRESS
RELEASES

STEVEN LEWIS

How to Write Perfect Press Releases
by
Steven Lewis

ISBN-13: 978-0980855968
ISBN-10: 0980855968

ABOUT THE AUTHOR

A journalist and writer for nearly 20 years, Steven Lewis has written for the *Financial Times*, *Esquire*, *GQ*, and the *International Herald Tribune*, among others. A long-time resident of Hong Kong, he had a popular and long-running consumer technology column in the *South China Morning Post* and was the technology editor of *Asian Business*.
He first published online in 1994 and today his titles are available in Amazon's Kindle store, Apple's iBookstore, and as audiobooks through Audible.
Steven is also a professional podcaster, ghostwriter and helps other writers publish their ebooks. His guides, reports, how-tos and blog can be found at Taleist (www.taleist.com).
He lives in Sydney with his wife and son.

HOW TO WRITE PERFECT PRESS RELEASES

CONTENTS

Introduction

In 1992 I left Oxford University with a law degree and no idea what I wanted to be except that it wasn't a lawyer and it wasn't going to be in the UK. Back in Hong Kong, where I'd grown up, I landed a job with a company that owned a chain of bar/restaurants.

My first task was coming up with a job title. I can't remember exactly what it was but it was hard because my job description was unspecific so it was something like "Executive". I do remember it was just the first of many made up and silly job titles I've had. After I became self-employed it was a long time before I stopped experimenting with "director", "managing director", "owner" and so on. Today I've settled proudly on "writer". One great thing about being young and having no experience in anything is that you might as well give one thing a go as another. My employer in 1992 needed publicity and, although I'd never written a press release, there was no reason not to give it a red hot go.

I wrote the release, stuck it in the fax machine (how 1992), dialled the number for the *South China Morning Post* and hit send.

I don't know what I was expecting; I certainly wasn't naive enough to think the editor of Rupert Murdoch's most profitable newspaper was going to get straight on the phone. When I heard nothing I assumed that would be the end of it. You can imagine my surprise to open the paper the following week to find a story about us on page 3. Not just a story, either. What appeared in print was my press release reproduced almost verbatim under the byline of one of the paper's journalists. The journalist had done nothing more than retype my release. The facts referenced in the release could have been completely untrue, and the people quoted might not have existed; nonetheless the piece appeared towards the front of Hong Kong's paper of record.

This was only the first time that happened to me. It's been happening ever since in other papers and in more than one country.

Rupert Murdoch has taught us since then that newspapers sometimes have far grubbier secrets than this one but this is the one that is important to you: newspapers are always looking for stories. Editors and journalists start every day with dozens of blank pages that must be filled by the end of the day. Journalists have too much space to fill in too short a period for every story to be one they happened on while pounding the pavement: they need a good percentage of their stories to come to them.

If you know how to package a story, you are a friend to the busy journalist. That isn't to say that every press release will find a home in print, either lifted verbatim or used as a springboard for a story a journalist writes herself. And you definitely won't see your story in print if you don't know how to package it. Journalists need stories to come to them because they're busy, far too busy to try to make sense of a bad press release. Don't grab them immediately? Deleted.

Here I speak from experience again. Several years after sending my first press release I became a freelance journalist. If nothing else it meant that what I wrote appeared under my own byline! (And most often in the same *South China Morning Post* that reprinted my first press release.) It also meant that I became the recipient of press releases, sometimes as many as 400 of them in a week. I saw the good, the bad and the truly execrable. Less than 10 per cent fell into the first category, which means you have a great chance of standing out if you know how to write a good press release.

Over the last 19 years I've made part of my living reading press releases as a journalist and writing them as a public relations (PR) person. Writing press releases is a craft. While it isn't a complicated one and it can be taught, there is a skill involved and pitfalls to avoid. This book will show you how to avoid the mistakes and write the best possible press release you can. It can't guarantee you a newspaper article, TV feature, or radio interview as a result, because nothing and no one can unless you marry a Kardashian.

Housekeeping

Throughout the book I use "publication" to mean newspapers, magazines, websites, TV and radio shows, blogs, podcasts and any other medium you might try to reach with a press release. This saves you ploughing through a few thousand extra words and some painfully constructed sentences. The principles of a good press release are identical regardless of the medium at which you're directing your information.

Also I will use "press release" primarily but interchangeably with "news release" and "media release". I favour "press release" because it's the most popular term despite the obvious anachronism. My actual preferred term is "media release" because there are more media out there than ever before. There's a lot to recommend "news release", too. It's a reminder that your press release should contain something resembling news or at least be of the moment.

Once through

I hope ideas will jump into your head as you read this. I encourage you to make notes as they come to you; but you should read the book through completely before you start writing your release. The sections build on each other and you'll find it easiest to start when you have the whole picture.

Case studies

The examples given in the book are a mix of real ones and ones that I've invented to demonstrate a point. Where the examples are real I've changed, or left out, enough details to protect the anonymity of the person and company concerned. The PR industry doesn't have a great reputation for ethics but it doesn't pay to kiss and tell. Some of these examples involve a few characters to whom I give names. They are fictional but based on real clients and experiences I have had.

George — the author

Not long ago I was asked to consult on the promotion of a self-published book. The author, "George", was towards the end of a long career in psychology in which he had coached high-profile business people. He had developed some new and interesting theories in the course of his career. Those theories and how he came by them were the subject of his book.

Doug — the lawyer

"Doug" is a composite of many of the lawyers with whom I've worked on PR. Doug is a senior partner in a large law firm. He is successful with clients at the big end of town but he's under constant pressure to bring in even more business. He and his partners see media coverage as important in raising their profiles among potential clients.

Kathryn — the pastry chef

"Kathryn" is a pastry chef who has worked in some of the best restaurants in the country. Having had a child, she wants to stop working nights and have the flexibility of her own business. She's moved back to her hometown to open a bakery and patisserie on the high street. She doesn't have a budget for advertising but wants to spread the word that she's open for business.

SECTION ONE
Developing the Right Mindset

The dirty secret of press releases

That some newspaper articles are little more — or nothing more — than rewrites of press releases is one of the dirty secrets of the media. Not so long ago readers of one of Sydney's local newspapers opened their newspapers to this story about a product my company, Taleist, had created.

Audio guide for ferry travellers

AN online publishing house has produced a 30-minute audio commentary for visitors using the Manly ferries.

The commentary has been produced by Taleist and can be used as an iPhone application, a downloadable MP3 or loaded on to a player.

Taleist founder Steven Lewis said the audio commentary is as much for the regular patrons of the ferries as it is for visitors.

People travelling on Manly ferries can now listen to an audio commentary during the trip.

"A million visitors take the Manly ferry every year," he said.

"Now they can turn that trip into a harbour cruise for only $9.99.

"The most frequent comment we get from Sydneysiders listening to our tours is: 'I didn't know that'.

"How many ferry passengers know, for instance, that there's a bit of the old GPO placed off Bradleys Head and that it's one end of the harbour's nautical-mile marker?"

The iPhone application, which includes historical images of Sydney, is available from the iTunes store for $9.99.

The audio commentary can also be downloaded from the Taleist website in MP3 format or a CD can be mailed, both for $9.99.

Loaded on a player from Taleist, the commentary costs $29.99.

Visit the Taleist website at www.taleist.com.

■ Readers of *The Manly Daily* can get a 10 per cent discount for purchases by using the code "manlydaily".

The article that resulted from my press release

Having read the article, take a look at the press release I sent the newspaper:

MEDIA RELEASE | 4 AUGUST 2010
New audio commentary for the Manly Ferry

Taleist, a new online publishing house, has launched its Manly Ferry Audio Commentary — as an iPhone app, downloadable MP3, or pre-loaded on a player. The commentary runs with the Sydney Ferries route from Circular Quay to Manly.

"A million visitors take the Manly Ferry every year. Now they can turn that trip into a harbour cruise for only $9.99," said Steven Lewis, founder of Taleist. "Sydney Ferries runs this amazing service but until now there was no way for passengers to know what they were looking at, all the points of interest and the great tales behind them."

The tour is as much for the 13 million local passengers as it is for visitors.

"The most frequent comment we get from Sydneysiders listening to our tours is, 'I didn't know that!'," said Lewis. "How many regular Manly Ferry passengers know, for instance, that there's a bit of the old GPO submerged off Bradleys Head and that it's one end of the harbour's nautical-mile marker?"

The iPhone app, which includes historical images of Sydney, is available from the iTunes store for $9.99.

From www.taleist.com, the Manly Ferry audio commentary can be downloaded in MP3-format, suitable for any digital player. It can also be mailed on CD. Both are $9.99.Pre-loaded on a player from taleist.com, the commentary costs $29.99.

For purchases from taleist.com, readers of the Manly Daily can get a 10% discount using the code "MANLYDAILY". (Not case sensitive.)

About us

Taleist (noun. teller of fine tales) is an online publishing company launched with three audio guides to Sydney: The Rocks, Opera House & Botanic Gardens, and the Manly Ferry Audio Commentary.
Steven Lewis is a professional writer with a background in travel journalism.
The Manly Ferry Audio Commentary is not affiliated with Sydney Ferries.

Contact

Steven Lewis 0415 826 100 | media@taleist.com

It looks familiar, doesn't it?

No one from the newspaper had spoken to me. They were working from the press release and a picture that I had sent them in the mail with a sample of the player.

The moral of the story

Prepare your press release like you are writing the article you're hoping to see in the publication because that might be exactly what you're doing.

Doing a good job

There are some points on which we should be absolutely clear. The first is that this doesn't show the newspaper is doing a bad job. It shows that I, as the PR person, was doing a good job. I had found the right story for the right publication and had sent it to the right person with the right information (and the right amount of it) to make an interesting story for their readers.

I had also made life as easy as possible for the journalist who put the story together. My version was written like a story, making it easy to reproduce as such with minimal extra work. It contained all the necessary information; and no time was wasted with unnecessary information. We know it contained all the information necessary because the paper was able to run it without contacting me for comment, verification or further information. If they'd needed to spend time doing that, my story might have been passed over in favour of one that was easier to write.

Just as important as saying what's necessary is not saying what doesn't need to be said but that will take up time, space and effort. This includes things your ego wants you to say but that have no chance of making it into a newspaper article.

To make things easier still for the paper I even enclosed a picture of the player, despite the fact that I'd included a player for them to see and photograph for themselves if need be. What if they had room for a picture in that week's paper but no time to take one? The story would have run without the eyeball-hijacking picture that led more readers to notice my story in the paper.

Although I wasn't known to anyone at the newspaper there were enough ways for them to check my bona fides sufficient to the risk in running the story. (Who would go to the trouble of writing and recording an audio tour and having it loaded onto a player if they didn't really exist as a business?) This was a fun lifestyle piece. How much critical attention would you realistically expect a journalist to give it? Everyone — reader, journalist and me — came out a winner. This lack of follow-up or fact-checking isn't going to be the case on every publication. Even in publications where it might happen, it's not going to happen in every section. A publication that rewrites a press release about an audio commentary for a ferry ride still isn't going to run a story about, say, a corrupt politician based solely on a media release.

As we've said already, every day journalists start with nothing and every night they put out a newspaper the length of a novel. Then they go home to get some sleep before they start all over again. That's a lot of blank pages to fill and some of what fills them is going to be triggered by, or sourced from, media releases. That means there is an opportunity for you provided you do it right. It does not mean that journalists are going to be grateful for any old rubbish you send to their inboxes.

The press release transaction

A press release is a transaction or at least the offer of a transaction: the mutually beneficial exchange of items of value. You are exchanging an idea for a story to run in a publication in return for being mentioned in the story. The journalist benefits because he needs to write good stories; you benefit from the exposure of being featured in a publication. The reader is not party to the transaction but has to benefit from it (by being informed or entertained) for the journalist to be able to write the story.

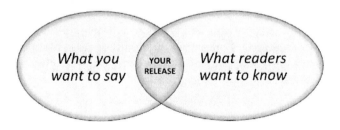

The press release transaction

While there has to be mutual benefit that doesn't mean the parties are equal. Most of the time the journalist is going to be the senior party in the transaction. Don't let that distract you from ensuring there is still benefit for you. Without it there's no point sending the press release. You should be clear, therefore, on what that value is to you. How would a story flowing from this media release help you achieve the goals you have set yourself?

I still write for publications and receive press releases but I'm also on the other side of the transaction as a business owner with products and services to promote. In that capacity I subscribe to a number of lists like HARO and SourceBottle that send out daily emails listing stories on which journalists are looking for sources. Often a journalist is writing a story for which I could be a source but appearing in that publication on that topic doesn't suit my own agenda. Seeing myself in print is a means to achieving something else, it isn't a goal by itself. I want to promote my services and products and raise my profile as an expert on particular topics. Being featured in an article where I'm not doing any of those things isn't worthwhile to me.

Recently I followed up on a journalist's request through SourceBottle to talk about email marketing. I was quoted extensively through the article as "Steven Lewis, owner of author coaching service Taleist". The article was about email marketing, not my author coaching service, but I still achieved a mention in a widely-read online and offline publication that will be seen by thousands of people, a decent chunk of whom are potential customers. Responding to the SourceBottle enquiry and the interview took about 20 minutes of my time.

A coincidence of wants

You're writing a press release because there's something you want to say, something that's important to you. Perhaps the biggest mistake I've seen press release authors make is not thinking beyond that and asking whether what they want to say is what anyone is interested in hearing. And not asking that question makes you no different from the dinner party bore who seems to think the whole room will be fascinated by him.

To write a press release that has any chance of success you must find the overlap between what you want to say and what a publication's readers will be interested in hearing. No one else is going to look for that overlap for you. That's because journalists don't care what you want to say, they care only about what their readers are interested in hearing.

In three minds

Any writing requires the author to get into the mind of the audience. To write a press release there are three minds you need to get into:

- The journalist's mind
- The mind of the publication's reader
- Your own mind

You'll have noticed where I've put those apostrophes. We're talking about being in the mind of *one* journalist and *one* publication's readers. We'll talk about this more later but it's important you understand you're writing a communication targeted to *a* journalist writing for *a* publication.

John Locke is a self-published author who sold a million books on Amazon's Kindle in five months. It made perfect sense for him to make his next book a guide aimed at self-publishing authors who would like to do the same. In the book he says that press releases never worked for him.

"In all," he writes, "more than 100,000 press releases have been sent on my behalf."

Does that sound like spam to you? It certainly does to me. It doesn't sound like anyone thought carefully about the needs of the journalist recipients of the press releases and the interests of their audiences. It sounds to me like someone thought about what it suited John Locke to say and proceeded to spray it out with a fire hose.

If that were a sensible strategy, why stop there? Why bother with journalists as intermediaries at all? Locke says he paid his publicist $7,500. The world abounds with dodgy characters who will email millions of people on your behalf for a fee. These characters are not so busy promoting Viagra that they wouldn't accept another $7,500 for promoting John Locke's books. Instead of spamming journalists, the author could have spammed readers directly.

I used to write a weekly column in the Sunday magazine of the *South China Morning Post*. The column was called Geek Chic and I wrote about websites and cool devices. It was clearly aimed at consumers. That didn't stop what sometimes seemed like every PR agency in town sending me press releases about IT from a business perspective.

Being interested in the iPad and what you can do with it is in a different universe from being interested in cost-saving refinements to Apple's supply chain management. Nonetheless I was forever being asked if I'd like to have lunch with Hewlett Packard's vice-president of printer sales to talk about the 12 per cent bump forecast for inkjet cartridge sales to small businesses. But my readers didn't care about that sort of thing. While *Vogue* is not going to write about the new sewing machines Chanel's seamstresses are using this season, however, somewhere there is a publication that might. The BBC used to have a wonderful program called *Newsstand*. Every week they would look at the magazines in a particular niche. It was unbelievable that every week they could come up with a different niche served by more than one magazine but they could. While on the trip that led to my book *The Ohakune Easter Hunt* I learned that New Zealand has not one but three magazines devoted to pig hunting even though its population is only the same as Kentucky's.

The trick is to get the right story to the right publication at the right time, not to throw 100,000 press releases out of a helicopter and hope a passing journalist picks one up.

The journalist

In the movies the journalist — in his uniform of trench coat and trilby — gets a tipoff from a source or overhears a whisper in a bar. The journalist of Hollywood's imagination doesn't write a story because the idea came to him in something as prosaic as a press release. The reality is somewhat less romantic than the film version. Many, if not most, of the stories you see in a publication will have started off as a suggestion from a PR person or someone acting as their own PR person. Even paparazzi are often tipped off by celebrities or their representatives.

Journalists are busy and, in the parlous state of the media market today, they're busier than ever because they're doing more with less. If they're on staff, they have an obligation to turn in a certain number of stories in a certain period. If they're freelance, they don't get paid if they don't turn in publishable stories; and the more stories they turn in, the more they get paid. Generally freelancers are also paid by the word. (True story: I got paid twice as much for writing "United Nations" in my stories as "UN".) I was talking to a fellow travel writer the other day. She'd just written something for a paper we'd both written for and she was paid the same rate per-word as they'd been paying for over 15 years! How much less does a dollar buy today than it did 15 years ago? This isn't a business where people earn enough to take their time.

This isn't to say that journalists are sitting there grabbing at press releases to rewrite. And it isn't to say that your press release is simply going to get dressed up into a story all about you. It might just be the acorn from which the story grows and your input will be part of a larger piece.

What journalists are looking for — all the time — is good story ideas. They're not looking for ways they can do you a favour and promote you or your service/product. But they do understand the trade: a good story for them to write in return for a promotional opportunity for you.

In writing a press release what you're doing is providing the idea for a story to a journalist who is busy and grateful for *good* story suggestions. If you give this a moment's thought, you'll see that this is very different from sending out an announcement of your latest achievement or product. Often you will not be the story, you'll be just part of it. People achieve things every day but you won't read about those achievements in even your local newspaper — "Janice Gets Promoted to VP Sales!" That's because those achievements, while understandably significant to you and those close to you, just aren't interesting to enough people.

The skill you're going to develop is making sure your story is interesting enough to make the papers and still includes an element of promotion for you.

Let's take our pastry chef, Kathryn, and her new bakery/patisserie. Outside the smallest towns this isn't really news because people are opening businesses all the time. But maybe Kathryn's new bakery/patisserie has a signature line of cupcakes, evidence of the exploding trend in cupcake consumption. If she pitches the story that cupcakes are the new big thing, she's positioning herself as an expert who can talk about that trend to the media. She is, after all, running her own bakery.

The story in the paper won't be about Kathryn's shop per se, it will be about cupcakes but Kathryn and her shop will get a big mention. The result is, therefore, the same as it would be if the story were just about Kathryn's patisserie: people are reading about the new shop in their newspaper. The difference is that readers are getting a story, not an advert.

There's an important distinction between PR and marketing. Marketing's job is to get people through the door of the bakery, e.g. by running advertisements or a direct mail campaign. PR's job is to increase recognition and reputation. That might lead to people walking through the door or buying something immediately but that's an ancillary benefit. If you go into the writing of a press release thinking like an advertiser, you're doomed. When writing your press release, therefore, getting in the mind of the journalist involves presenting your information as the idea for a story, not as copy for an advertisement.

Like I say, the journalist is busy, he's only going to give you and your release a fraction of his attention. That means your release has to jump up and paint him a picture of what his story will look like if he writes it.

When writing your press release, you need to be asking yourself:

If I were this journalist, would I understand immediately what would be in it for me and my readers if I were to write this story?

The reader

Journalists write for readers. When putting your press release together you need to know who those readers are. When the journalist picks up your press release, he's asking, "Is this going to be interesting to my readers?" So you have to have asked — and answered — that question for yourself first.

Working out who reads a publication isn't hard to do if you check it out. You won't have to spend too long with a particular publication to work out whether it's aimed at men, women or both and their:

- Age
- Education level
- Interests
- Aspirations
- World views
- Social standing
- Economic situation

It's not hard to see, for instance, that Socialist Worker and Vanity Fair are aimed at different audiences.

No publication or show is aimed at everyone because, if they were, they wouldn't reach anyone. Every publication has a target market; and comprehensive publications, like a Sunday newspaper, will have target niche audiences for each of their sections.

It might be harder to work out the target market if you've never seen the publication; but, if you can't work that out, why are you sending the publication a press release? If you don't know a publication's target market, how can you possibly know that it's the right market for your story? If you think everybody in the world will be interested in your product/service — or should be — it's a sensible marketing plan you need before you consider a press release.

If you're having trouble working out the target market of the publication, get onto the website and find the section where they talk to advertisers. Here you'll find a media kit, or the opportunity to send off for one, which will give you all the demographics. The publication will tell you exactly whom they reach because they want to convince advertisers that their audience is the right audience for what they're thinking about advertising.

Incidentally, this is another reason to make sure you're not thinking like an advertiser when you write your press release. If your press release looks like advertising, you'll soon find yourself referred to the advertising department and invited to pay for space.

An example

The media kit for Wired tells us the vast majority of its readers are 34-44 year-old male college graduates now in professional or management roles earning an average of $94,000. It tells us all this and more in some detail (down to a decimal place on most metrics).

The magazine chooses to describe its content through this quotation from AdWeek:

"…an editorial mix spanning technology, business, science, entertainment, and culture — in essence, becoming the chronicler of this decade."

It took me just a couple of minutes to find all that online but it's a priceless trove of information when it comes to building a picture of Wired's readers and their interests. From there I can see what sort of stories will, and won't, work for Wired.

Once you know who a publication's readers are you can start getting into their heads and asking what you can tell them — through the journalist — that will be interesting to them and useful to you. Also you might realise you'd be wasting your time with this publication as it doesn't reach the people you thought it did.

Your own mindset

Finally, you need to get into your own head and make sure you're in the right mindset before you write your press release.

Hopefully you're passionate about your story and believe that you're helping out the journalist and providing something of interest to his readers. That doesn't mean, however, that you're the one doing the journalist and her readers a favour. If you go into this believing that you're giving a gift rather than receiving one, it's less likely to go well for you.

Unless you're Octomom or you've landed a 747 on the

Hudson, you're asking journalists for a favour, not doing them one. Even if you're still convinced that you're the one doing the favour, you need to know that this is extremely unlikely to be the way the journalist is looking at your transaction.

This mentality runs through the whole thing: you're providing a service and you need to make it as easy as possible for the journalist to take you up on your offer. Any hurdle you put in the way — being obscure, being difficult to get hold of, asking too much etc. — could be one hurdle too many.

You also need to be clear on why you are writing the press release and be realistic about what to expect. If you have a product or a service and are asking for a review, you might get one but you might not like it. If you're looking to be interviewed on a topic because you have something to say — because you have products or services in the relevant area — you might get a mention but not an endorsement, e.g. "… said Steven Lewis, author of *Perfect Press Releases*" rather than "Steven Lewis who is an expert on writing press releases and whose excellent book on the topic can be found on Amazon.com".

You might also propose a whole story, e.g. an interview with you on the art of writing press releases, and find you're just part of an article that takes the story in a different direction, e.g. a piece about using the media in your promotional activities. You might even find your story idea translates into an article that also references your competitors. The journalist's job is to write something interesting to his readers, not to reward you for your hard work with an exclusive puff piece.

SECTION TWO
Profiling Your Targets

Be selective

There are websites that promise you they will distribute your media release to thousands of outlets and journalists, sometimes for a fee, sometimes for free. Mostly (or maybe always) this is rubbish. For a start by "distribute" they mean they're going to upload your release to their website. Journalists have never been more short of time or had more abundant sources of information. To anyone who has worked in or with the media it's ridiculous to suggest there is some magical website scoured by journalists willing to take a generic press release then re-imagine its content in a form that works for their publication. When I worked at a newspaper many releases would arrive by fax. I used to wonder what the local PRs would think if they could see this machine that simply scrolled thermal paper into a box on the ground, often until it just ran out of paper.

If you're a journalist, you have relationships with good PR people who know who you are and are sending you stories tailored to your needs. You don't need to be sifting through an undifferentiated slush pile of releases that have gone through no quality control to get on the website. They're there only because someone's paid to stick them up on a website. It's the 21st century equivalent of the old fax machine scrolling unaddressed faxes to the floor.

It's your job, as the person with the story to sell, to find the right person to get it to. This involves profiling two things:
- Publications
- Journalists

Fitting your story to the publication

It should probably go without saying that the story you come up with has to fit with the publication in question. My experience on the receiving end of press releases tells me that it is worth mentioning, however. When our lawyer, Doug, had a story about property law we didn't send it to *Men's Health*, but I'll bet *Men's Health* gets plenty of press releases that have them wondering how anyone thinks they might be of interest to readers looking for stories relevant to their health.

It helps, as it always helps, to put yourself in the reader's shoes. Fix in your mind the story you're pitching. Now imagine yourself as a reader of the publication. You open the publication up one day to find this story. Does the story fit with the rest of what you've been reading in the magazine? Or is it somewhat jarring to go from *Perfect Abs in a Weekend* to a story headlined *Building Codes Changing in February*? This exercise will help you to focus on matching your angle to the publication.

Make a list of the publications you'd like to be featured in — the ones your potential customers and clients are influenced by. Then look through them to see if they feature articles analogous to the one you're proposing they write. Some stories won't make it into some publications regardless of what you do. Other times, however, it's a case of tailoring the story to fit the publication.

A hypothetical example

Anne is a 29 year-old accountant who recently ended a 10-year relationship. The break-up made her re-evaluate her life and her goals. She remembered she'd always said she'd write a novel one day. Deciding this was that day, she arranged with her firm to take a six-month sabbatical to do just that. She's now self-published her book on Amazon and is looking for some media coverage to help with sales. Her ideal reader is like her: a young professional female.

Anne decides she's going to try two very different publications: *Cosmo* and an industry magazine for accountants. Both these publications might be interested in Anne's story but they'll want to come at it from different perspectives.

1. *Cosmo* might be interested in the story of how one woman turned heartbreak into creative inspiration and used it as a springboard to realise a life goal.
2. The trade publication might be interested in how Anne's firm supported work/life balance by allowing her that six month sabbatical to try something creative.

In both these cases Anne and her book might not be enough of a story on their own. She might have to think of a way to suggest a story in which she is just a part. *Cosmo* might want to write a broader feature looking at several women who've turned a setback into a leap forward. Equally the trade publication might want to take a more general look at a trend and speak to other accountants who are creating a work/life balance in interesting ways.

It might sound counterintuitive, but Anne should think about whether she can find some more examples to package with her press release to make it even easier for the journalist to picture his story. She might herself find and list five other women who used their imaginations after a break-up; or five other accountants doing something unusual with their time and the support of their firms. Yes, she'd be dividing the coverage over a number of other people but she'd be increasing her chances of there being coverage in the first place.

Neither story in either publication would be directly about Anne's book but both would expose her book to readers of the magazine, which is her number one goal.

Taking this approach means Anne is going to have to write two different press releases. This is undoubtedly more work than writing one and sending it out to as many places as you can think of. The question you must ask yourself is whether you want to do a little work that will likely achieve nothing or a bit more work so you stand a chance of getting what you were after.

Fitting your story to the journalist

Fitting your story to the publication is the first step. The second step isn't essential but it does increase your chances of success: it's targeting the right section of the publication and, if possible, the individual journalist. The fax machine at the newspaper that used to scroll releases endlessly into a box on the floor was checked periodically by an intern. Releases addressed to an individual would be taken to that individual. The rest were left to fall into the box on the floor and that included releases addressed to "the editor".

It's tempting to send releases to the "the editor", but that's only fine if the publication is small. When you're pitching to a publication with dozens or hundreds of staff spread over multiple floors, writing to "the editor" looks lazy. If *you* can't be bothered to narrow it down better than that, why would the publication bother to employ someone to do it on your behalf? Writing to, say, "the CEO" might be forgivable when you're writing to a company whose organisational structure you don't know and couldn't reasonably be expected to find out. The structure of a publication is hardly a mystery to people on the outside, however. You can read all about it every day, week or month. I answered the phone at a magazine once to be asked by a PR intern who our "books editor" was. If she'd just glanced at the magazine she'd have seen we didn't have one. If I were a client of her agency, I'd be nervous about putting my brand in the hands of PR people who don't even know how to read a masthead.

As I mentioned, one thing I did as a journalist was to

review gadgets, which meant I was interested in some things that technology companies had to say but not others. I was, for instance, interested in the launch of a new digital camera, but I wouldn't have been interested in hearing how many had been sold or were forecast to be sold. In both cases the story is the digital camera but the perspective is completely different:

How cool is this thing to use?

VS

How many of these things are going to sell?

The PR agency for a technology company had, therefore, to be careful in segmenting its list of journalists. To some PR companies we might all be "technology journalists" but reviewing products and writing about the companies that make them are chalk and cheese, especially to readers. When you turn to Roger Ebert you expect film reviews not an analysis of the balance sheet of 20th Century Fox.

At a minimum you ought to know what section you're pitching to be in. You must know if this is a sports story, a lifestyle story, or one for the gardening section... If it's a sports story and you can't think of the journalist most likely to be interested, at least send it to the editor of the sports section rather than the editor of the whole publication. Section editors are frequently listed in the publication's masthead, either in an edition or on the website.

If this all sounds like hard work, good because it is and it should be. That publications are discerning about what they write and where they put it is what makes editorial so much more valuable than advertising. If the publication you want to appear in isn't discriminating about what it writes and for whom, the publication probably isn't worth appearing in.

You might be frustrated and thinking that surely a journalist to whom the story isn't appropriate would at least know whom it might be right for and pass it on. He won't. The reason is the same: who is doing whom the favour? Even if one journalist's trash is another journalist's treasure, it's your job to find the one for whom it's treasure.

It's your job to match story to angle to publication to section to journalist. Whatever you think about it, that's just the way it is.

How to pick a journalist

You've chosen a publication because its topics and audience overlap with yours. Ideally you'd narrow your search even further to a specific journalist. Do you see the same journalist's byline cropping up in the section that's right for you? Does it seem like your story might fit in with the sorts of things she writes about? A large percentage of journalists are freelance, which means they work for themselves and not for particular publications. Most of them will have websites. These are a wonderful resource for you because here in her own words the journalist will be articulating exactly what she wants to write about.

Freelancers are also great to target because they write for more than one publication. If they don't think your story is right for the publication you're targeting they might suggest they write the story for another publication.

When you find a journalist you think might fit with your story, Google her for more clues. Just as you imagined opening a publication to see your story there, imagine this journalist writing your story. Having read some of her other pieces can you imagine her writing a piece about you?

Rub on a small patch first

Some products advise you to try them out on a small patch of fabric to make sure they don't do any harm. It's good advice for a media campaign, too.

Depending on the size of your story, you might want to select a few journalists or publications to send it to first. This has a couple of advantages:

1. Publications don't generally want to be running the same story as their competitors, so if you find one that is interested you'll probably need to stop there anyway.
2. You can learn from your mistakes — if you don't get a response to the first batch of releases, take another look and rethink.

Don't ignore bloggers

Don't ignore the power of blogs. My metro newspaper has a readership of nearly 800,000 people but they're a diverse group. For the most part they've really only got two things in common: they live in the same city and they read newspapers. That means only a subset of those 800,000 readers will be interested in any one story. Also, the day's paper that carries my story will be in the recycling bin tomorrow. There's an online edition that lives longer, which is great, but that version most likely won't link to my website because newspapers are bad internet citizens in that way: they don't like to send traffic anywhere else. Someone who reads the story online in the newspaper and is interested in finding out more about me will have to get onto Google to find me. The more hoops people have to jump through, the less likely they are to start jumping.

Bloggers, on the other hand, generally have smaller audiences but the members of that audience share a common interest. Even though the total readership is smaller, my story on a blog might actually be read by more people who match the description of whom I'm trying to reach. Additionally, the blogger will likely link to my site, which will send me traffic as well as improve my site's relevance in Google's eyes. And blog posts stay online (with those links) forever.

You'll read plenty about how bloggers need to be approached differently from journalists. PR people have been banging on about this for years. Their concerns arise because bloggers are sometimes not shy about publicly ridiculing clumsy PR attempts. Journalists don't do that publicly. Good PR people have, however, never been worried because the skills that make them good at working with journalists make them good at working with bloggers.

What irritates bloggers is to get generic releases that have clearly been sent to dozens or hundreds of bloggers. When you do this — to journalists as well as bloggers — it says "I can't be bothered to refine this distribution list", which is the same as "I don't care if I'm wasting your time". Put another way: it's spam.

Unfortunately there are bloggers who are just as silly in their own way. They think anyone who has the temerity to contact them should be a lifelong devotee of their blog, familiar with their every post and peccadillo. If the blogger wrote in February 2001 that he doesn't like getting press releases on a Wednesday, you should know that, and woe betide you when your release hits his inbox on hump day. This is immature and most bloggers aren't like that. They expect what journalists expect: that you've contacted them because you know something about them, their work, and what interests their readers.

Learning about the blogger is easy to do. On the whole blogs have one author, who will have profiled himself or herself somewhere on the site; and you have access to all their writing so you can easily get a feel for what it is they're interested in. Some of the bigger blogs will also have sections detailing how they're willing to be approached and about what. Again, it might be troublesome to have to submit your information in different ways for different blogs, but remember it's not you doing the favour.

Explain yourself

Where bloggers are different is that they aren't usually professional in that blogging isn't their main source of income. Blogging might not even make them any money at all. Journalists are, however, doing their job and part of that job is getting press releases so they're used to it. They are used to the clunky style that comes from trying to pack facts into a contrived format. Bloggers, on the other hand, might have different expertise and not be as familiar with the impersonal style of press releases. Blogging is a more connected, more personal way of communicating than journalism. When sending a release to a blogger, therefore, you might want to make a more personal approach by, say, including a cover letter explaining why you thought the blogger would be interested in the release, e.g.:

Dear Steven,

I've noticed that you've written several times about topic X. I especially enjoyed your observation in [TITLE OF BLOGPOST]. It made me think you might be interested in...

Please, please be authentic. If you're going to write something along those lines, there must be a genuine link between what you've said you've enjoyed and what is being covered in your release. Your blogger might not be a professional writer but they didn't build a big enough audience to be interesting to you by being an idiot.

It's still a transaction

The idea of the press release transaction applies to bloggers, too. There needs to be an overlap between what you want to say and what a blogger's readers want to read about.

My Taleist blog is aimed at authors who self-publish their work, so I write about news that affects self-publishing authors and about ways they can self-publish to greater effect. Every so often, however, I'll get an email from an author just shouting the name of his book. This one is a real example reproduced here in full:

"Howdy! I'm an 8-time produced screenwriter who's entered a new realm of writing. I just published my first ebook, [Name of Book]. It concerns an 18-year old man who takes on a gang of Vietnam vets who have slaughtered his family. Here's the link: [link]"

And here's another one (again reproduced in full):

"Editors,

How about checking out the Kindle book [name of book]?"

That one didn't even include a link to the book. Its author thought I (or my "editors") would search Amazon for his book and write about it.

Why?

If either of these authors had looked at the Taleist blog for longer than it took to find my email address, they would have seen that the blog isn't just a list of all the books in the world that have been published. No blogger could hope to keep up with a list like that. It would take a team of people typing constantly just to write out the titles. And why would anyone read this list? I couldn't even list all the books published by my readers: they're *all* writing books!

But this isn't a reason for either of my two correspondents to accept defeat. Looking at the Taleist blog closer they would have seen that I do run guest posts from authors who have advice to offer others. Perhaps my correspondents had learned something in the process of publishing their books that would have been useful to share with my readers. In return for writing 400 to 800 words about their lessons, they would have exposed their book to my readers, which is what they wanted. It would have been more work than just emailing me the name of their book but it would have had an actual result. We'll discuss this sort of oblique approach in the next section.

SECTION THREE
Working the Angles

Angles

We talked earlier about Anne, the accountant who took time off to write a book. Her story was of interest to two magazines but they each had different takes on it. The women's magazine wanted other examples of women who'd turned heartbreak into triumph. The trade publication wanted to write about the trend for young professionals to want more balance in their lives. These differences in approach are "angles" on the story.

The angle is the point of view from which you look at a story. Every story you'll ever read in a publication has an angle, a way of taking a story and presenting it in a way that answers these questions that readers might have:

1. Why are you writing this story now?
2. Why is it in this publication and this section of the publication?
3. So what? (Why should I, a reader of this publication, care about this story?)

The "now" factor

Question One goes back to why I like "news release" as a term. To a greater or lesser degree every story in a publication has an element of "now" about it, a reason why it is in this edition, not the one before, the next one, or one at some other point in the future. This is most apparent in the current affairs section of a newspaper — the paper is writing about this battle or this weather event because it has just happened. You can see the "now" question answered everywhere in a publication, however. Even this week's recipes are chosen not only because they're tasty but because they match this season — salads for summer, hot food for winter, in-season vegetables, etc. Can you imagine the food editor of a New York magazine running soup recipes in August? When you're writing your news release remember to get across why your story is relevant right now (even if it's a bit of a stretch it's better than nothing).

At one happy point in my career I was being paid thousands of dollars by one of the world's largest PR agencies to write press releases on a freelance basis for a global technology company. One day my client, the account manager at the PR agency, told me the IT company was concerned that the press releases being sent on its behalf weren't resulting in any media coverage. The PR man was calling me to ask if I had any idea why that might be.

"It's because your news releases don't contain any news," I said.

I was just the copywriter, not the person charged with creating the IT company's PR strategy. I wasn't anywhere near those meetings. To be honest it had never occurred to me that senior managers at an international PR agency wouldn't know they were putting out information that would never be picked up by any media outlet. I'd presumed it was just a box everyone knew they were ticking. Press release sent. Check. Copy on our website. Check.

What is an angle?

Starting out as a journalist I found the idea of an "angle" the hardest thing to grasp. I'd want to write a story because the subject interested me. Let's say I loved the idea of going to Paris to write about it. My pitch to the editor would basically be "Steven goes to Paris, has a look round, has a jolly time, then writes about Paris to pay for it all." My editor would ask me what my angle was. "Paris" might be your story but you need a lens through which to filter Paris to have a manageable story that's worth printing.

It took a while but I learned that an angle is the way you approach a story to decide what should be in it and what should be left out. If you don't have an angle from which to write your travel story about Paris, how do you not end up not including everything but a street directory? An angle is the difference between a travel feature and a child's list-making approach to "What I did in my summer holiday" — we stayed in a hotel, we had breakfast, we caught a train, we went to a museum, the paintings were nice, Daddy ate a croissant, then we went to the Champs Elysee...

In the case of Paris you might write about Paris as seen from a bus or a bicycle or a hot air balloon. You might write about Paris through the lens of its food — what would a day's breakfast, lunch and dinner in Paris look like? You might come at the story from the angle of something that's happening right now: the spring collections are launching in a month, what's going to be hot to do in Paris during the shows? By having an angle you know what to include in the story and what to leave out.

Angles can be seen at work most clearly in the biggest stories. Was there, for instance, a publication in the world that didn't write about the wedding of Prince William to Kate Middleton? For each publication, section, section editor and journalist to justify jumping on the bandwagon they had to have an angle that made sense to their specific subject area.

The news reporters covered the "news" angle — what's just been announced or discovered about the wedding. The fashion reporters covered the dress, the shoes, the bridesmaids' dresses. The business reporters covered the effect on commerce and the economy. Foreign editors wrote about how the wedding was being received overseas. Travel writers wrote about Royal London, the palaces, the changing of the guard, where the royals eat... Trade magazines covered the wedding in a way that was relevant to the industries they covered — what glassware will be used at the reception (for journals for glass manufacturers); how the spike in passengers was being handled by airlines (for air industry journals)... Finally, journalists working on the media sections — the part of the paper where journalists write about their own industry — wrote about how all their colleagues were covering the wedding.

Conversely, a fashion section wouldn't have written about the cake; or a travel section about the dress, etc.

The angle has to answer the question of why the reader of that publication or that part of the publication would be seeing a story about the royal wedding. Next time you open a publication look for the angles. Try, for instance, looking at the travel section. Is what you're reading just an article about Bali, or is it an article about Bali for families, or Bali for couples, or Bali for lovers of Asian culture?

As you look through the magazines you'll see also that not every angle on a story will work for every publication. A magazine that writes from a human interest perspective is not going to cover a story from the same angles as a news magazine. Imagine how differently Oprah's *O* magazine would have covered the aftermath of Hurricane Katrina from, say, *The Economist*. Same story, different lens through which to view it, which means different things to include and leave out.

When thinking about an angle on your story, you have to do what accountant Anne did in Section Two — Profiling Your Targets. You have to come up with an angle that will work for each publication or group of publications you've identified.

Finding an angle

Because a press release is about selling the journalist a vision of what his story is going to look like, you need to have an angle, too. When it comes to a story like a royal wedding finding an angle is easy but what about on a less global story?

Let's say our lawyer, Doug, has a practice in construction law and new legislation is pending. Doug wants to put out a media release introducing himself as an expert who could comment on the new law. That answers the question of what's in it for Doug to speak to the media. It doesn't answer the question of what's in it for a journalist to talk to Doug or for his readers to hear about it.

You need to give journalists a sense of the story you're suggesting, which means you need an angle on the legislation — because "New Law Coming" might be a story but it's not one that needs expert comment from Doug.

The following are all possible angles for a story about the legislation that would require interviewing someone:

- It's great legislation because…
- It's flawed legislation because…
- It will impact a certain type of business in a way those businesspeople should know about (e.g. contractors will need to train their workers in a certain way; developers will need to wait three months longer for permits)

An angle doesn't have to be weighty, something of tremendous import. If we go back to our example of Kathryn's new patisserie on Main Street, what sort of angle might we have there? Perhaps you would focus on the energy of the shop — "New bakery brings colour and fun back to Main Street". Or the angle might be about the Kathryn's qualifications and the benefit to the town — "Award-winning pastry chef brings her art to town".

The world is angular

Finding an angle is like riding a bike: it's easy when you know how but it might seem like you're not going to get it at first.

Where I grew up there's been an annual charity go-kart race for a long time. It's great fun — teams build weird and wonderful pedal karts and race them round a city park for 24 hours to raise money. One year the organisers called me as a journalist hoping I would write a story about that year's grand prix for the newspaper. Unfortunately I couldn't because they weren't pitching me an angle I could use.

The organiser was understandably disappointed so I tried to explain to him that I needed an angle to justify writing the story. In the first year for instance it would have been easy: the angle would have been that someone had found a new and wacky way to raise money for a good cause. In the second year the angle might have been that the event had been so successful it was now twice the size.

He felt that it should be enough that the event raised lots of money every year but the harsh truth is that thousands of people in every city raise millions of dollars every year. A newspaper can't write about all of those people and events. It needs a reason to be writing about this charitable event at this particular time.

The organiser sighed and told me it was getting harder and harder to run this event every year.

"Ah, is the event in danger of folding?" I asked him.

Despite the difficulties there was no danger of the event not happening, he told me. That's a shame, I said, because that would have been an angle: "Successful Fundraiser in Danger of Closing After 13 Years".

If I'd had the time perhaps I could have worked with him on his angle but I didn't. And it's not the journalist's job to do that with your press release, either. You need to work out the angle and present it. The journalist might read your press release and come up with a different angle, but that's another matter. You need to suggest one.

Should you find yourself struggling to find an angle, remember the world isn't round after all. It's made up of edges and corners. There will *always* be an angle on a story. Just think about the variety of reactions your group of friends would have to anything that happens in the world.

An example of angles in the real world

Your mutual friend John, a father of two, divorced six months ago and now has a new girlfriend, Sarah, who is significantly younger than he is. You're at a dinner party with several of your friends. John isn't there but he becomes the topic of conversation. It seems all your friends have a different lens through which they're looking at John and Sarah's relationship.

"How soon is too soon to start a relationship after a divorce?" wonders Jane, who wears her moral compass on her sleeve.

"Do relationships work when there is a big age gap?" asks Mike, whose office recently gained an intern from the local college.

"What are the potential pitfalls of introducing your kids to a new partner?" is the question on the mind of Tom, a divorced father.

"Sarah is horrible because…" is the view of Jim, who has always been the catty one in your group, which is why everyone wants to sit next to him tonight.

That's one story — John has a new girlfriend — but four different angles on it.

Oblique angles

Apple has worked hard to produce exciting and exquisite products and it reaps the rewards in terms of an easy life when it wants its products in the media. A new iPad comes out and the media is clamouring to talk about it. Apple's invitation to the launch of its new iPad in

March 2012 said only "We have something you really have to see. And touch." They didn't need to say anything else because the mere fact there's a new product from Apple is enough to justify writing a story: the iPad *is* the story, its newness, sexiness and desirability is the angle. No technology publication could afford *not* to report on it.

When you don't have that sort of place in the public consciousness, a product, service or pronouncement from you won't generate media coverage just because it comes from you. This is the position in which 99.9 per cent of the media-seeking world finds itself. As a result you might not be able to come directly at what you want to talk about, you might have to be a little creative in how you approach it.

Let's take our author, George, as an example in this case. George has a product — his book — that he wants the world to know about. The first draft of his press release ran along the lines of "George has published a book". Over a million books are published annually in the US alone. That's the best part of 3,000 books a day in just one country. It isn't news that you've published a book, unless you're famous and even then only if you're spilling some beans. Understandably George wasn't thinking about the other 999,999 other books. He'd found writing his book difficult and it had taken him years. On top of that he'd self-published, so he'd also had to learn how to get a book designed, printed in Asia, and distributed to bookshops. None of that had been easy either.

That George could place a copy of his hardcover book in my hand was a monumental feat in George's world and, therefore, headline news. And because this was headline news in George's life he couldn't see that this was of no interest to people outside his circle. If he'd thought about it, he'd have realised he wouldn't want to open his newspaper to find a story every time someone had learned to play the piano or to change a car tyre. Things that are major achievements for individuals are mostly everyday achievements in the world.

Because George's book wasn't a story in itself, he needed to look for an oblique angle. He needed to find a way of looking at it so that his book wasn't the story but it was part of another story. George needed to take a step back from the actual production of the book and focus on what the book was about. He had interesting theories on coaching high profile businesspeople to greater levels of success. He could have written a press release about:

- The current business climate and the difference between the way winning business leaders approach difficult economies compared to their weaker counterparts.
- How coaching senior executives helps companies come out on top in the bad times.

If the story had been picked up by a publication, the result to George would have been about the same: a chance for readers of the publication to hear about George's book. That chance would just have been wrapped in a story about something broader than his book.

Finding a hook

So the truth is that you're not always going to be the story. The reason, for instance, the PR agency wasn't getting any media coverage for their technology client was because they had me write a press release every time the client made a large sale. But you don't read in your local paper an article every time someone drives a BMW off the lot of your local auto dealer, even if they've bought two.

Sometimes the fact is that something that is important to you isn't going to be important to the media or its readers; or not important enough, anyway. In both cases you might have to settle for taking out an ad if you really must see it in print.

One of my most vivid recollections of my time doing PR for the lawyers was my boss getting Doug to walk over to the window with her. He'd called us to a meeting to tell us that the firm had just taken on a new lawyer in his area. He wanted us to send a press release to the financial papers.

"Do you see all the offices out there, Doug?" my boss said. "In every one of those offices someone started work today and someone is finishing. You won't read about it in tomorrow's paper and you wouldn't want to, which is why no one is going to read about your new hire tomorrow either."

When I worked with Doug and his colleagues this was a constant battle. Because the firm had decided that media was an important part of business development, they wanted to be in the media all the time. Our job was to find things that were happening –– economic events, new legislation, corporate trends and so on –– on which our lawyers could take a position. These things were "hooks" on which a journalist could hang a story and Doug could hang an opinion.

If we go back to what I call the press release transaction, our side of it worked in this case like so:

- We functioned as an extra pair of eyes for journalists, looking out the trends that might make for interesting articles (hooks on which a journalist could hang a story).
- We packaged the trend into a press release, including what our lawyers could add as comment — "Town Hall issuing building permits too fast," says local lawyer Doug, cautioning that due process is not being observed.

The press release gave the journalist an idea for a story and at least one person who could serve as a source. Often we were quite aware that the journalist would have to seek additional comment for this story. Our work might have benefited someone we weren't working for but we were just happy to be manufacturing a story in which our guys could appear.

As in any press release transaction the journalist and his readers got an interesting story, and we got a mention.

If you're running a PR campaign and you expect to be the story rather than a voice in the story, you face a steeper uphill battle than you need to; and you're likely to get less coverage than you would if you take a more realistic approach.

You should be always on the lookout for news in your area — trends, reports being published, major happenings. Don't think that every dress designer or cake maker mentioned in the coverage of the 2011 Royal Wedding was contacted first by the media. Most will have contacted the publication offering their take on the wedding from a particular angle.

SECTION FOUR
Writing Your Release

The writing mindset

We talked in Chapter One about the three minds you need to be in: the journalist's, the reader's and your own. Now we need to focus on the last one: your mindset. Athletes get into a winning frame of mind before each race, concentrating on what makes them great, that core of self-belief. This isn't quite that, but you should remind yourself before you start writing that:

- This is a great story
- You are the right person to tell it

Any doubt you have will come through in the writing so don't have any!

Answer these questions on a piece of paper before you start:

- Why is this a great story for this publication?
- Why am I the right person to tell it?
- If the reader were to take just one thing from this story, what would I want it to be?

You don't need to write much, just a couple of words to remind you of your answers.

After you've finished writing the release you'll go back and review what you've written against these bullet points. You will be amazed at how easy it is to go off on a tangent when you're writing the release and not cover what were — and still are — so clearly the points you *should* be highlighting.

The anatomy of a press release

Our author, George, was set on having media coverage as a part of his book promotion strategy so he'd already written his press release by the time I met with him. There were two main problems with the draft. The first was a case of Small World Syndrome. We'll talk about that more later. For now suffice it to say that George needed to shift the emphasis from the fact that he'd published a book. He needed to give the journalist a flavour of all the great insights he had into an interesting subject after years of unique experiences up close with business leaders. For the release to have a chance of being picked up by a publication it had to be about what the readers of the publication wanted to know: how to do better in business (and where to find a book that could help).

The second problem was also to do with the content, not its substance but the way it was presented.

"I spent a long time on Google," George said. "There were a lot of conflicting suggestions but one thing every site agreed on was that a press release shouldn't be more than a page."

That's good advice, but unfortunately George's first solution had been to shrink the font size to the point that anyone over 35 would have needed a magnifying glass to read it.

Size does matter

The references George had found to a one-page press release were references to succinctness, not the size of the print. It's a great rule of thumb: if you've written more than a page, you've probably written too much. In that case go back and check whether every word is necessary. You can't cheat by shrinking the font by a point or two to get the release down to one page. Better a legible release that flows onto a second page than a font size small enough to get the Bible on a grain of rice.

As an editor the first thing I do when given a printed document is ask the author what it's about, what it's supposed to achieve, and for whom it's been written. They're often surprised when I hand the printout straight back unread and tell them it's at least 40 per cent too long.

I don't need to read a document to know it's too long, if I know the audience and how much time they have on their hands for this subject. It doesn't matter how good your argument is if someone doesn't have time or patience to read it at the length at which you've expressed it.

The foundation step in writing a concise press release is to be crystal clear *before* you start on what it is you want to say. Really think about this before you put fingers to keyboard. There should be no more than three points you are trying to get across. Any more than that is confusing, and some of the points will get lost so just pick your top two or three.

Layout

It would be easier if there were rules, a single template to work from. Because there aren't, you need to be clear on what press releases are supposed to achieve in order to write in a format that works to do that. In this aspect a press release shouldn't be any more daunting than preparing an invitation to a party. An invitation can come in almost any form you could conceive of — an embossed card, an e-mail, a phone call or a ransom note telling you when to leave the money in the park. Whatever the form chosen, the purpose of the invitation — getting people to a certain place at a certain time for a certain reason — dictates that you'll want to include particular pieces of information in a way that makes them easy to extract, e.g. time, location, and requirements (like dress code or bring a bottle).

The purpose of your press release is to paint a picture of what the eventual story could look like; provide key details of what you can add to the story; and let the recipients know where you can be found.

As with an invitation there are standard elements to be included, however you choose to lay them out. They are:
- Headline

- Contact details
- Date
- An about section
- Key pertinent data, e.g. dates, times, places, titles, numbers and so on
- The body section — the bit where you write your story
- Quotations

If you have those things and they are easy for the reader to extract, you don't need to get too hung up on the format.

By "easy to extract" I mean that the journalist should be able to see what your media release is about at first glance, i.e. spot your headline. If that grabs his attention, he will look at the body of your press release, which he'll find because it's the bulk of the words. If he grabs it later to use to research or write the story, he should be able to spot things like your contact details easily.

Let's look at those elements one by one.

Headline

This is arguably the most important part of the whole release. If your headline doesn't sell your story, the rest of your release is unlikely to get read. Would you carry on reading an unsolicited document if the title didn't interest you?

You're looking for something interesting but not obscure. It's the balance between a headline that gives the journalist a vision of the story you're suggesting and something that's too much work to decipher. Remember, the more work you ask someone to do, the more likely your request is to end up in the too-hard basket.

For Kathryn's patisserie/bakery, for instance, "Something Sweet on Main Street" is an interesting headline but possibly too much work; maybe there's not enough there for me to be certain I'll get a payoff for reading on. "New bakery brings something sweet to Main Street" gives the same flavour but more detail the journalist can use to decide whether to continue reading.

You might think I'm splitting hairs but remember how your press release is being delivered. Only if you're faxing or mailing it will the body of the release be just a downward glance from the headline. If you're emailing it, which is most likely, the headline will be the subject line of your email (discussed later). It might be all the journalist has to go on when deciding whether to click to open or delete.

And frankly, even if you are posting or faxing, it's still easy enough to bin a release without reading more than the headline. I've held many press releases in my hand, glanced at the headline and put them down without reading any further.

Date

The date should be near the top of your press release. The most common place for it is on the same line as the first sentence. It's there so the journalist is absolutely certain he's dealing with something current.

Usually the information in a press release can be used by a publication any time from the date it was released. Some people like to put "for immediate release" across the top of a press release but that's redundant. A "news" release is, by definition, for immediate release in the absence of any indication to the contrary. If you send a journalist something, she's certainly not going to be phoning you to check if it's okay for her to use the information because you didn't put "for immediate release" on it.

If you don't want the media to use the information right away, don't send the press release until you *are* ready. It isn't the media's job to run a filing and diary system for your information. From their point of view, they're doing you a favour and aren't going to go out of their way to do it for you.

That said, sometimes a media release is "embargoed", which means the information in it isn't to be used by a publication beforehand. A company might, for instance, want to give the media plenty of time to prepare for an upcoming event but not want the media to use the information before the launch. Say, for instance, it's a "surprise" that your event is going to be opened by a Hollywood star. You don't want to ruin the surprise for the public so you don't want that information in the media beforehand. You do, however, want the media to send people to your opening, which they're more likely to do if they know someone newsworthy will be there.

Be thoughtful about embargoing things, though. It's something to be used where there's a good reason (one that the journalist is going to understand, not just one that suits you for personal reasons). If you send a journalist material that's embargoed, you're creating more work for him — diarising the embargo date, etc. — so he's not going to do it unless it's a great story and there's a clear reason. A story he might have written if he'd got a standard press release might not get written if you've made it unnecessarily hard.

Previously an embargo would only have been for the biggest of happenings, events the media might need time to prepare to cover but which the author of the release wanted to keep from the public until a certain time. An actor might, for instance, agree to an in-depth profile to be published only when his latest film is released.

Timing was easier to manage before the internet. Monthly magazines have lead times measured in months so you could tell them something in January, confident you wouldn't see it before March or April. These days they often have a companion website so you might need to specify an embargo date even for a monthly.

Most press release authors, however, should be thrilled if their press release gets picked up at all, not worrying about exact timing.

Contact details

If a journalist wants to contact you about your release, he will expect to get hold of you quickly. This might be because he is on a deadline; he might just be impatient for whatever reason; and he most definitely will think he's doing you a favour, so he might move on if you make it hard to get hold of you. Your release might have sold him on a story idea but, if you're not around to answer questions, he can find someone else to comment for his story or drop it and move on.

Personal contact details should be given for the responsible person — direct email address and direct phone number (preferably for the phone that's in your pocket at all times). Don't send your press release on company letterhead and think the journalist will guess whom he should be calling, or will take time to work with the switchboard operator.

Alternatively, you might provide direct contact details for someone else, a person more likely to be free to answer the phone or their email and who, when contacted, has the connections, influence and ability to make the rest of it happen, e.g. to hunt the CEO down to return the journalist's phone call a.s.a.p.

Do not send out a press release if the talent isn't going to be available to answer follow-up questions quickly. By sending the release in the first place, you've implied that you're available to provide comment. When I work with clients I always impress this on them: if you're not willing to drop what you're doing to answer a follow-up enquiry you might blow your one opportunity and hurt future opportunities. If a journalist likes your story and has convinced an editor of its merit, she now has to write it. If she can't get hold of you, she'll find someone else to comment or tell the editor it didn't work out and get onto the next story.

The contact details would normally be in the top corner of the release or at the very bottom. For example:

For more details contact:
Kathryn Campbell
Phone: +61 413 829 909
Email: kathryn@sweettreats.com
Postal addresses are not necessary. If there's to be follow-up, it will be by phone or email.

The body of the release

This is the meat of the matter, your chance to present your story. We'll talk about how you do that later. For our purposes here we'll just say that this is your "story". In it you're going to combine facts and figures in a compelling package.

The first paragraph

The blog TMZ was the media outlet that broke the news about Michael Jackson's death. The entire first paragraph of their story is:

Michael suffered a cardiac arrest earlier this afternoon at his Holmby Hills home and paramedics were unable to revive him. We're told when paramedics arrived Jackson had no pulse and they never got a pulse back.

In those 36 words you get a rehash of the headline — Jackson is dead — and 10 more facts:
1. It was a heart attack
2. It happened this afternoon
3. He was at home
4. He lived in Holmby Hills
5. Paramedics were called
6. They came
7. Jackson had no pulse when they did
8. They tried to revive him
9. It didn't work for even a second
10. TMZ wasn't there but is getting information from

someone in the know

That's about one fact every three words.

The first paragraph of your release needs to be similarly compact and full of the most important information. No one finishes everything they start reading, which is why information is in descending order of importance. Don't make the mistake of falling into linear story telling, something we'll talk about later:

"Five years ago Steve Jobs had an idea..." is the start of a linear story. What Steve Jobs was doing five years ago is not the lead and it doesn't help with our "now" factor. "Today Apple launched the iPod, the most advanced MP3 player on the market and the future of music sales" is the lead. A few paragraphs later in the release we might learn that Steve Jobs' idea was five years in the making, but that's not the most important part of the story because the lead is of course the arrival of the iPod, the rest is just background.

Quotations

None of us speaks naturally in a way that lends itself to a newspaper quotation. Think about how neat and tidy the quotations are in newspapers and magazines. None of the ums, ers, subclauses and circumlocutions in which we actually speak. If journalists faithfully transcribed speech without nipping, tucking and paraphrasing, our favourite publications would be longer and less readable. Politicians, and those who are going to be recorded live by cameras and microphones, are trained to have a couple of perfectly formed remarks that can be cut out neatly. That's what a sound bite is.

Potted quotations in press releases make the journalist's job easier because you've already crafted an eloquent sentence or two. The journalist now has something to decorate and break up his story without having to coax something equally eloquent from you "live". That isn't to say the journalist isn't going to speak to you and include some of what you actually said, if that suits him. Even when they have interviewed a source, however, journalists will often return to the tidy quotations in the original media release when they're appropriate.

Quotations colour a newspaper story, making it more interesting than if it were just the reporter telling his readers something. That's why quotations are something you should give a journalist, especially if you might only be part of the story.

It's more than possible that a journalist who quotes someone has not spoken directly to him or her on the topic. It happens all the time. It might be misleading but it's not dishonest: it is genuinely something the talent said, they just didn't say it to that particular journalist in person. (Even more truthfully, they might never have said it and, in the case of someone incredibly busy, they might not even have seen it but they at least won't deny saying it!)

The first quotation in your press release would usually be the second or third paragraph.

You can have quotations in a story from more than one person, but only do it if there's a very good reason. You want your story to be as simple as possible and one voice telling it helps to keep things uncomplicated.

An about section

After the body of most press releases there will be an "About" section. This is where you would put information about you, or your company, that might be useful background for the journalist.

This, for instance, is what appears at the bottom of every media release from Coca-Cola regardless of the subject:

About The Coca-Cola Company
The Coca-Cola Company (NYSE: KO) is the world's largest beverage company, refreshing consumers with more than 500 sparkling and still brands. Led by Coca-Cola, the world's most

valuable brand, the Company's portfolio features 15 billion dollar brands including Diet Coke, Fanta, Sprite, Coca-Cola Zero, vitaminwater, Powerade, Minute Maid, Simply and Georgia. Globally, we are the No. 1 provider of sparkling beverages, juices and juice drinks and ready-to-drink teas and coffees. Through the world's largest beverage distribution system, consumers in more than 200 countries enjoy the Company's beverages at a rate of 1.7 billion servings a day. With an enduring commitment to building sustainable communities, our Company is focused on initiatives that reduce our environmental footprint, support active, healthy living, create a safe, inclusive work environment for our associates, and enhance the economic development of the communities where we operate. For more information about our Company, please visit our website at www.thecoca-colacompany.com.

Here's the same from FedEx

About FedEx Corp.
FedEx Corp. (NYSE: FDX) provides customers and businesses worldwide with a broad portfolio of transportation, e-commerce and business services. With annual revenues of $39 billion, the company offers integrated business applications through operating companies competing collectively and managed collaboratively, under the respected FedEx brand. Consistently ranked among the world's most admired and trusted employers, FedEx inspires its more than 290,000 team members to remain "absolutely, positively" focused on safety, the highest ethical and professional standards and the needs of their customers and communities. For more information, visit news.fedex.com.

You'll find the same if you Google any company and the phrase "press release".

If the release profiles a particular voice, you might also have a section about that person, e.g.

About Steven Lewis
Steven Lewis has moved between journalism and public

relations throughout a 20 year career on two continents. He is the author of several books and the internationally-read Taleist blog (www.taleist.com).

This would be too much information to put in the body of the press release with your story but it is information the journalist might want if he does write something. In the internet age he could look it up but your job is to remove as much resistance as possible. Fortune favours those who make life easy for journalists.

In your case you might change the "about" information depending on the subject of the release. I would, for instance, change mine depending on whether I was issuing a release about, say, this book or one of my travel books.

It also counts towards your one page total!

Example

Earlier I gave you the example of a press release about Taleist's audio commentary for the Manly Ferry. Let's look at it again in the context of what we've just talked about.

Firstly, the whole release is 317 words and, with logo and letterhead, takes up just under one A4 page in a 12-point font. It is packed with facts and information useful to a journalist who was going to write a story based on it. I challenge you to find anything extraneous, anything that has no chance of helping the journalist put the story together. I'm not saying you can't do it but take note of how hard you have to look.

1. MEDIA RELEASE | 4 AUGUST 2010

2. New audio commentary for the Manly Ferry

3. Taleist, a new online publishing house, has launched its Manly Ferry Audio Commentary -- as an iPhone app, downloadable MP3, or pre-loaded on a player. The commentary runs with the Sydney Ferries route from Circular Quay to Manly.

4. "A million visitors take the Manly Ferry every year. Now they can turn that trip into a harbour cruise for only $9.99," said Steven Lewis, founder of Taleist. "Sydney Ferries runs this amazing service but until now there was no way for passengers to know what they were looking at, all the points of interest and the great tales behind them."

5. The tour is as much for the 13 million local passengers as it is for visitors.

6. "The most frequent comment we get from Sydneysiders listening to our tours is, 'I didn't know that!'," said Lewis. "How many regular Manly Ferry passengers know, for instance, that there's a bit of the old GPO submerged off Bradleys Head and that it's one end of the harbour's nautical-mile marker?"

7. The iPhone app, which includes historical images of Sydney, is available from the iTunes store for $9.99.

8. From www.taleist.com, the Manly Ferry audio commentary can be downloaded in MP3-format, suitable for any digital player. It can also be mailed on CD. Both are $9.99. Pre-loaded on a player from taleist.com, the commentary costs $29.99.

9. For purchases from taleist.com, readers of the Manly Daily can get a 10% discount using the code "MANLYDAILY". (Not case sensitive.)

10. About us

Taleist (noun. teller of fine tales) is an online publishing company launched with three audio guides to Sydney: The Rocks, Opera House & Botanic Gardens, and the Manly Ferry Audio Commentary.

Steven Lewis is a professional writer with a background in travel journalism.

The Manly Ferry Audio Commentary is not affiliated with Sydney Ferries.

11. Contact

Steven Lewis 0444 844 944 | steven@taleist.com

1. The date

There it is, nice and prominent. I sent this release in the

post because I was including a player. By making the date prominent the journalist who opened it could be confident this was a story for *now*,not outdated because the package had got lost in the post for a while.

2. The headline

I'm extremely proud of this particular product and it would have been easy to wax lyrical about it, indulging myself with references to working hard for months or doing a wonderful job but that wasn't the lead. The lead is that there's new commentary to go with the Manly Ferry ride and that's what the headline says.

This isn't a cute or intriguing headline. For this release I knew that a simple fact would do the job. The newspaper felt the same, running the story under a similar headline: "Audio guide for ferry travellers".

3. The first paragraph

Note how the first paragraph expands on the headline. We don't go into genesis mode — how I had the idea, when I had the idea, what I did to make this audio commentary happen. We get the key details: a bit more about who did what exactly.

4. The first quotation

Here's a quotation for the journalist to use in the story, which is what he did. Note that the quotation is still laser-focussed on relevant information. There's colour here — about points of interest and great tales — but several facts are also in what I'm saying. If the journalist doesn't use the quotation, he still knows how many tourists take the ferry annually, the price of the commentary, and that this is a first.

Just because it's a quotation don't waste it, make every word count whether it's used as a quotation or in another way in the newspaper article.

The rest of the release

5. Another useful fact.

6. This is a colourful quotation but see how it sells the

product. With the nugget of trivia about the GPO marker this quotation is begging to be used in the article. And it was.

7-9 This information is crucial to me — where can you buy the commentary and in what form — but less important than the rest of the information to the "story" I'm selling in this press release — that there's a commentary to be bought in the first place. That's why it's last. Everything in a press release is important — or it should be left out — but there is still a hierarchy and some is less important than others.

10. About us

This background could have been useful in the story or it might just help the journalist see this as a serious business from someone with some credentials.

11. Contact details

Easy to find from the release at a glance and also direct to me, no switchboard, no landlines. You could reach me wherever I was.

Don't bury the lead

The worst thing a journalist can do is "bury the lead". The "lead" is the key aspect of the story, the one piece of knowledge the reader absolutely can't do without.

Think of how you read a newspaper. You're not going to read every word, which means you'll see more headlines than first paragraphs. You'll also read more first paragraphs than second paragraphs and so on. This is because you won't start reading every story, and you won't finish every story you start. For this reason the most important information — the lead — has to be at the top. The information that follows it will be arranged in decreasing order of importance.

A reader who flips through a newspaper reading only the headlines will have a good overview of the state of the world — a riot here, an earthquake there, a tax rise coming and so on.

You can see this structure — key facts at the top, lesser facts lower down — in any news story you read, but one of the easiest types of story in which you can break this down is the obituary. To see this in action let's go back to website TMZ's story about Michael Jackson.

Which of these options do you think was the actual TMZ headline?

- *Celebrity Singer Dead*
- *Fatal Heart Attack Recorded*
- *Ambulance Called to Holmby Hills*
- *Three Children Fatherless*
- *La Toya Jackson Visits UCLA Hospital*
- *Michael Jackson Dies*

It was, of course, the last one. It's not witty, clever or intriguing but it does give you the lead, the one absolutely crucial piece of information in the story. All of the headlines suggested above give you facts, all of which are included in the TMZ story, but the last one is the most important.

The whole TMZ story is just 158 words and, if the three-word headline grabbed you, the 36-word first paragraph would tell you:

- It happened today
- It was a heart attack
- He was at home in Holmby Hills when it happened
- He was dead before paramedics got there

If you stopped reading now, you'd still have a significant amount of information, enough to clue you in on what's being discussed around the water cooler.

You need to have the same focus on the lead when writing your press release. Go back to what you did first in this process: you decided what it is that you have to say that a publication's readers might be interested in hearing. This is your lead, don't bury it. You'd be amazed by how many do.

Let's look at the whole of the story as it appeared in

TMZ.

The original TMZ story

Michael Jackson Dies

We've just learned Michael Jackson has died. He was 50.

Michael suffered a cardiac arrest earlier this afternoon at his Holmby Hills home and paramedics were unable to revive him. We're told when paramedics arrived Jackson had no pulse and they never got a pulse back.

A source tells us Jackson was dead when paramedics arrived. A cardiologist at UCLA tells TMZ Jackson died of cardiac arrest.

Once at the hospital, the staff tried to resuscitate him but he was completely unresponsive.

A source inside the hospital told us there was "absolute chaos" after Jackson arrived. People who were with the singer were screaming, "You've got to save him! You've got to save him!"

We're told one of the staff members at Jackson's home called 911.

La Toya ran in the hospital sobbing after Jackson was pronounced dead.

Michael is survived by three children: Michael Joseph Jackson, Jr., Paris Michael Katherine Jackson and Prince "Blanket" Michael Jackson II.

An alternative version

Here's another way to tell the same story with exactly the same facts but with the lead buried.

Fatal Heart Attack Recorded

A staff member at a Holmby Hills home today used the 911 emergency service to call paramedics to attend the 50 year old father of three children, Michael, Paris and Prince.

The emergency medics found no pulse when they arrived and

were unable to get one back on their way to the hospital.
Hospital staff were also unable to get any response when they
tried to resuscitate the patient.

The man is said by a cardiologist at UCLA to have suffered a
cardiac arrest.

Friends and the man's sister La Toya were distraught at the
hospital.

The dead man's name was Michael Jackson.

It seems ridiculous, doesn't it? If you were writing this story, of course you would know to spit out right at the top that Michael Jackson was dead! That's easy to see in this case because it's a dramatic story but every story has a lead (or it's not a story) and you'd be amazed how many press release writers bury it.

Why we bury the lead

To avoid burying the lead in your press release it helps to think about why it might happen. These are two of the most significant reasons.

1. A preference for linear storytelling in writing

We tend to tell stories in a linear fashion when we're writing them down.

"Today I went to the grocery store to get some food for the party and some things happened to me in the following order…"

But this isn't how we tell stories when we're talking aloud. This is probably because we're taught how to tell stories in writing, so we revert to the formal styles we learned at school. When it comes to oral storytelling we revert to our natural instincts, which are far better in this regard.

"My car was stolen at the grocery store today. I'd gone to get food for the party…"

Or, less dramatically:

"This lady in the grocery store was rude to me today. I was there to get food for the party and…"

The car wasn't stolen and the lady wasn't rude at the chronological start of your story but those are the facts you would lead with, which is why they're called the lead.

Listen to your friends speak and you'll hear that we often give our stories headlines unconsciously. "A Terrible Thing Happened to Me at the Grocery Store Today…" or "My Car was Stolen Today…" The first thing we say when we think of a story to tell in conversation is often like a headline. Then we proceed with the rest of the story.

2. Small World Syndrome

Working in PR for one of the large law firms, my boss and I would be called at least once a year by Doug's secretary. Doug wanted us to know that he was travelling to London so we could alert the *Times*, the UK's paper of record on legal matters. It wasn't that Doug had a particular story to tell them, he felt his presence in London *was* the story. Doug was suffering from what I call Small World Syndrome. In his world his international travel was a big deal, and he wasn't able to see that it was not of significance outside his circle. Doug's position in the firm and the firm's culture made it impossible — or at least unwise — to explain to him that what he was asking was akin to a high school glee club alerting *Rolling Stone* to their end-of-year performance.

You might find yourself in the same predicament. The star of your press release is the big boss or someone senior. Inside an organisation it can become reflexive — or a matter of survival — to act as if every movement or thought of this person is a matter of significance. It follows naturally that you might treat your story as if its lead is the mere fact that it comes from or is about this person. In the wider world, however, the reading public isn't necessarily in awe of your boss. They won't treat his or her every pronouncement with the gravity it is accorded by those whose mortgages, health care and school fees he or she influences.

Perhaps you are sending the press release on your own behalf, in which case you must ask yourself whether you are being objective about what should be the lead.

I don't mean to suggest that an individual's thoughts or pronouncements will never be newsworthy. If Mark Zuckerberg has anything at all to say about the state of social media, for instance, people will listen. In fact they'd pay to listen. You just need to be sure to go back to the press release transaction, and make sure what you're saying falls in the sweet spot between what you want to talk about and what a publication's readers want to hear about.

The conversation test

Both an instinct for linear storytelling and Small World Syndrome can be tackled with the Conversation Test. Imagine you're telling your story to a friend who doesn't work for your company. What information would you be leading with? When writing your media release remember those storytelling instincts, perhaps pretend you're having a conversation with a friend while you write.

Run the test again after you've written your first draft. Go back to the picture of your friend in your mind. Does the release you've written still reflect the way you would present a friend with the story if you were in conversation?

Note also that we tend to explain the "now" factor to our friends. When we're telling them a story we instinctively say why we're telling it at this point in time:

"*That* reminds me…"

"An odd thing happened to me *today…*"

As you think about telling your friends the story in your press release, ask yourself whether you've answered the "now" question.

Follow the lead

The lead is going to shine through your headline, your first paragraph and that first quotation. It's your *key* key message, if you will. It probably won't be your only key message, however. Your key messages are the most important pieces of information you want to get across. Three is probably the maximum number of key messages you could hope to see conveyed in one story. In my audio player example, for instance, they were:

- There was now an audio commentary for the Manly Ferry
- It was available in a number of formats
- It was entertaining for locals and visitors alike

You might be able to get more than just the lead in the first paragraph, but in what follows the first paragraph, the body of your release, you need to make sure you get them all across. Just as in the example I gave you with my audio player media release everything proceeds in diminishing order of importance. If the information in your fifth paragraph is more important than the information in your fourth paragraph, you need to swap them round.

I can't tell you what to put in those quotations and paragraphs because I don't know what your story is. All I can tell you is to think about exactly what you're trying to get across, and to choose every word to help you tell that story. Keep your ego out of it because you are not the target reader, you have to limit what you write to what is interesting to the readers of the publication.

Press releases often sound unnatural because every word has to count, and you're trying to get as many facts as possible into as few words as possible. That's okay.

You're not actually writing the newspaper story. Even if a journalist uses your release as the bulk of their story, they'll rub off its stilted edges. Your job with the release is to convey facts while giving the journalist a sense of what their story will look like. If you're stuck here, go back to the example release and see again how I tell a story while packing the facts in there. I've deconstructed it for you, so you could always write your press release to exactly my model. Look at each of my paragraphs and match them to your story.

If you would like to use my press release as a example to follow, it's available to you for download from Taleist.com at http://l.taleist.com/m.

If you're still blocked at this point, my advice is to just start writing. No one is looking, no one needs to see your first attempts if you don't want them to. A journey of a thousand miles begins with one step. Every piece of writing begins with getting that first word on the blank page. Write something, anything. Scribble some headlines down, write some bullet points of what you want to say, mind map the key elements of your story.

To help you focus on what's important we'll play a mind game. Imagine you're in the offices of a newspaper. It's a large publication so it takes up the whole floor of a skyscraper. At one end of the floor is a shredder. Your press release has been fed into the shredder so the first words that will be shredded come from the bottom of the page. The last thing that will be shredded will be the headline. At the other end of the floor is your target journalist, who has to write his whole story based only on the material he can save from the teeth of the shredder. When I say "Go!" my assistant is going to start the shredder. At the same time the journalist is going to start running to grab your press release before it's completely destroyed. We know it's going to take him at least a few seconds to sprint from one end of the floor to the other. That means you're definitely going to lose some of your release before he can get to the stop button. As he can only use the material he saves, you want to be absolutely certain that it's the least important information at the bottom so that's all he'd lose access to.

Read your release again to be certain everything is in order of priority.

First draft

It's time to write that first draft now you have clarity about:

- Your target publication and journalist
- Your angle
- Your lead
- Your other key messages
- Why your story is a "now" story
- The structure of a press release

Checklist

What follows is a checklist to make sure you've covered everything you should have covered. Also your first draft will probably be longer than a page. Following the checklist will help you to cut it down.

Meeting your own expectations

Look back at the piece of paper on which you answered the questions:

- Why is this a great story for this publication?
- Why would the publication write about it now?
- Why am I the right person to tell it?
- If the reader were to take just one thing from this story, what would I want it to be?

Does your first draft answer all of these questions

clearly?

Keeping the lead at the top

The last question identifies the lead, the single most important part of your story. Is the lead at the top or is it buried?

Key messages

Are all of your key messages covered in the release? Do they stand out above all else? If a friend who knew nothing about the content beforehand read your release, would she walk away after reading it with your key messages in her head?

The headline

Does your headline stand out? It should reflect the lead and pique the reader's interest.

The first paragraph

The first paragraph should be the lead writ large. Are you sure you've got the most important facts here and nothing extraneous? Remember, your story shouldn't be linear. Start with what's most crucial and finish with what's least crucial.

Quotations

Have you included some interesting quotations the journalist can use to bring some human colour to the story? Do those quotations sell your story? Can the content of the quotation be used in an eventual story whether or not it's used as a quotation? How many people have you quoted? If it's more than one, does that unnecessarily complicate the story?

Less is more

Look for superfluous words. You'll be amazed by how many there are. "We are currently working on…" means exactly the same as "we are working on" except it's 25 per cent longer. That might not seem a lot but it adds up as one sentence piles onto another. I'll bet you can go through your press release draft at least four times before you've found every extraneous word.

In the reader's shoes

Finally, put yourself in the shoes of the readers of your target publications. Being as objective as you can, is this something you can imagine being interested in if you were a paying reader of the publications you're aiming at?

What to include with your release

Few, if any, of the product shots you see in publications are taken by the publications themselves. The easier you make it for a publication to put a story together, the higher your success rate will be.

As a travel writer I'm usually met at check-in by someone from hotel management. The best hotel PRs will have prepared a pack that includes facts about the hotel and professional photographs. It always amuses me to find in the pack a headshot of the general manager. Have you ever read a travel story illustrated with a studio shot of the Swiss-trained general manager? But better to have too much to offer than too little.

If you *are* the story you're selling, it might be appropriate to have a picture of you available. In fact try to have a couple in different styles, perhaps one against a background that could be cropped out and one with more character. There might be other pictures that would help, too. Unless they're just to help the journalist with research, these will need to be publication quality, i.e. crisp and high-resolution.

Releasing
the
Release

Your email

I'm old enough to have received the odd press release in the mail; then it was by fax; and then by email. Back in the day those first emailed releases came through my dial-up modem, so it was inconvenient when emails included large attachments that could take several minutes to download. What was "large" in those days isn't necessarily large today of course. Today we can assume at least that a journalist is on a broadband internet connection. They are still short of time, however, so you need to think through the way to be most helpful. For that reason I still wouldn't send large attachments. The journalist could, for instance, be checking email on her mobile phone, not the faster office connection. Even today many organisations have surprisingly tight limits on the size of email attachments that will get through their system. Consider also the number, as well as the size, of attachments and don't include many. The journalist's email software might just arrange them in alphabetical order, which means they have to sort through them to see what they should be clicking first. My advice is to limit your email to the text of your media release. You can provide links to where the journalist can download photographs, supporting documents and so on. This uncluttered look comes across as more professional and less demanding than one that arrives with lots of bits and pieces to sort through.

Speaking of uncluttered, make "information at a glance" your aim. Your story will get more consideration if it's easy to see what it is quickly, rather if it's presented as a jigsaw puzzle that needs assembling. I was always surprised how many PR people would choose as their subject line "Press release" and include the actual release as an attachment with a name like "Release v02.doc". This meant I had to double-click to open the email and double-click again to open the release *just to find out what it was about.* That's a lot of clicking to ask of someone who is busy and who might not trust that it'll be worth it. Deleting is, after all, just one click.

I can see some people might think that advice above is silly because my suggestion here wouldn't seem likely to save all that much time per email. If you feel that way, I ask you only to consider two things. The first is how much time you would save over 20 or 50 emails per day on top of all the other emails you receive. The second is your own behaviour when screening email. For instance, perhaps there are emails you subscribe to and often take time to read but sometimes you will delete them because you don't have time or capacity to take in that day's issue. Deleting those emails to make room in your inbox seems productive even though it might have taken only a minute or two to read — or at least skim — them.

The press releases that are most likely to get read are the ones where:

- The headline of the press release is the subject line of the email
- The body of the email is the rest of the press release
- No double clicking required, easy to scan.

Because all the text is in the email and not an attachment, it will be easier to find by a journalist who remembers getting it and who uses the search function on their email software for key words. To make it even easier to see key information at a glance you might try a light touch of boldface for emphasis, but don't go mad with different fonts, sizes and colours. Journalists deal with plenty of crazy people so don't do yourself a disservice by looking like one because your email looks like a ransom note.

If you don't have the technical know-how to store your collateral online and provide links, include only the bare minimum with your email. You can mention what else you have so the journalist knows you have it should they want to ask for it — "Images available on request".

Remember the primary purpose of the release is to sketch a picture of the finished story for the journalist. Your goal is to whet their appetite, not to cover every possible eventuality or question in one email. If you try to be too comprehensive, it's going to make it harder to hit that one-page target. If the story appeals, the journalist can work with you to get what she needs.

Finally, send one email per journalist. You might not be personalising the email and just cutting and pasting but it doesn't look good to send an email that's blind copied to any number of people or, worse, has a load of competitors in the To line. Barbara Walters doesn't need to see that Diane Sawyer is getting the same email.

To follow up or not to follow up

There are two schools of thought on whether you should follow up a media release or not. As a journalist I hate it when PR people phone me to ask if I received their media release. Email is almost 100 per cent reliable so it's a fair assumption that I did get it; and, if I didn't contact you, I'm not interested. When you're getting hundreds of releases a week, you could spend your whole time on the phone acknowledging receipt. Of course I didn't feel that way about everyone. There are some great PR people who are a delight to talk to, and who could sometimes convince me that I was wrong about their release. I was always happy to hear from them; many became clients; and some became good friends. That's a relationship thing, though. We had a relationship and they used that as a reason to call, not an administrative chase — often done by the most junior person in the office — which was a waste of both our time.

Colleagues I respect, however, swear by the follow-up. My guess is that this is because they are following up journalists with whom they have the relationship I describe above.

If you do follow-up by phone, you'll need to decide what to do if you get voicemail. Personally, I prefer not to leave a voicemail and to keep calling back until I get the journalist on the phone. If I leave a voicemail and don't get a reply, I have to decide whether to follow-up the voicemail if I don't hear anything. Then I'd be following up a voicemail that was following up an email; and no one wants to look like a stalker.

How to avoid following up at all

There is one way you can definitely avoid following up and that's to make a pre-emptive phone call. It might sound contradictory for me to be recommending a phone call when I've just said phoning is a bad idea in my opinion. The calls I don't like, however, are the ones chasing me to ask if I received something. Those calls make me feel like I'm helping you with your admin. The call I'm recommending is the first contact: your pitch on the phone is the first the journalist will have heard of your story idea. If he or she likes it, you've got your press release ready to email them immediately as follow-up.

A call tells the journalist you know who they are and what they're interested in. It also suggests they might be the only person you're calling, giving them the right of first refusal. It would be spectacularly bad form to call a journalist to offer a story, have them accept your offer, then offer it round to others. You'll only get away with that once. This way, therefore, you could save yourself a lot of blind mailing: pick your first choice journalist, call and you might have to send only one press release.

In my opinion this is the best approach of all. This can be daunting, which is one reason why you shouldn't do it before you have written your press release in the way we've talked about in this book. That's because, after you've gone through the process laid out here, you'll be absolutely clear about your story, your angle, your lead and your key messages. And you have it all written down in front of you. You have, therefore, everything you need to sell the story in a short conversation. If the journalist is interested, you can follow up instantly by emailing the release. This way you know it will get opened, because it's actually requested and expected. You might also find the journalist isn't interested in this story or angle but is working on something else or has another idea you could help with. They might also make a note of you as a possible source for future stories. If you've identified your journalist correctly, i.e. he's someone who writes about topics you're a good source on, this would make sense.

I know I said the pre-emptive call was a way to avoid following up, and hopefully it is. However, if the journalist you've spoken to doesn't reply after you've sent the release, he'll understand completely when you call after a reasonable period of time to inquire if he's still interested. It's okay to follow-up in this circumstance because you're building on the budding relationship you formed in your first call. Journalists are not horrible people, they're just busy. They do know they need people like you suggesting good stories to them; and you know this journalist thought your story had potential, so you know you're in good standing with him.

Tracking your campaign

Make a note of when you send each release, and to whom, so you can track how long it's been. A spreadsheet is perfect for this.

Don't forget to check the publications, too. Many times I've sent out a release and heard nothing until I saw the story in the paper. During the course of writing this book, I replied to a journalist's request on SourceBottle for people with expertise in online marketing to comment on trends for the year ahead. I jotted down some thoughts, sent them off and didn't hear anything. Journalists' names don't show up with their requests on SourceBottle. They don't have to give the names of the publications they're writing for either; in those cases you get a generic description like "freelance" or "national magazine". As a result you don't even know where you should be looking for the article. That's why I have Google Alerts on my name and my company name, Taleist. I'd forgotten all about this particular exchange when I had a pleasant surprise in the form of a Google Alert telling me I was quoted in *Smart Company*.

This is a final illustration of who thinks they're doing whom a favour in the media transaction. This journalist was aware that none of us who replied knew her name, so we had no way of contacting her to ask if she had used our material. She knew also that we didn't know what publication she was writing for, so we couldn't even check it when it hit the newsstands. Nonetheless, she didn't feel obliged to tell us where our comments would be used, let alone thank us for our time. If *Smart Company* were a print-only publication, I might never have found out. That's the nature of the media beast.

SECTION SIX
Conclusion

The chain of success

A prospective client once asked me if I would handle their public relations on a success fee basis. I would get paid only if the work I did with them resulted in media coverage. I told him I didn't work on that basis and didn't know anyone in PR who did. I explained to him that success fees work only when success is within the control of the consultant. In the case of public relations it isn't. I might work with his company to see if they had any media-worthy stories. I couldn't be responsible if they had nothing to say that would interest readers, but I would still have done the work investigating. If they did have a story, I would have to identify suitable publications. Having done that work, it might be that I couldn't raise their interest. The publications might already have run a similar story or be working on one; this story might fit the publication but not the editorial calendar they'd planned out; or they might see how it could fit but just not be interested. If I successfully matched a publication to the story, I would work with the company's spokesman to talk to the journalist. The spokesman they chose might not have what it takes to "sell" the story or fumble the interview on the day. Or he might ace it, and the journalist might write the story, but the space set aside for the story is lost to coverage of a bigger story. I don't mean to trivialise, but imagine how much great PR work was lost when publications gave over huge amounts of space for weeks to coverage of 9/11 or the Asian tsunami. Stories are written but not actually published all the time for reasons that have nothing to do with the quality of the story.

I tell you this to point out there are many links in the chain of successful public relations that are beyond your control. If your first press release doesn't get traction, don't give up. Yes, publications have pages and pages to fill with each issue but there is no shortage of people pitching ideas to fill them. This book has given all the tools you need to write a perfect press release but the recipe still needs a generous dollop of luck and good timing to succeed.

I wish you all the luck and serendipity you need to see your story in the publications of your choice

.

Also by Steven Lewis...

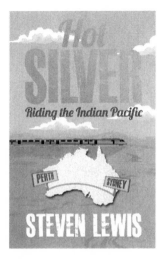

It's Bill Bryson meets Paul Theroux in Steven Lewis's hilarious review of his train journey across Australia on the Indian Pacific in the train's fortieth anniversary year.

Hot Silver stops with the train in Broken Hill, Adelaide and Kalgoorlie, all of which are closed when the Indian Pacific visits. Most closed of all, though, is Cook, the tiny town (pop. 5) in the middle of the vast Nullarbor Plain, 200,000 square kilometres of nothingness in the centre of Australia.

A perfect read for the armchair traveller, *Hot Silver* is a laugh-out-loud account that brings to life one of the world's most famous train trips with the deft sketches and first-hand observation of a seasoned travel writer.

AVAILABLE FROM AMAZON

Spread your message with social media...

Facebook, Twitter, LinkedIn, and blogging have changed the media landscape forever. In this four-week email course, you'll learn for each:

1. **The opportunity** — a simple explanation
2. **How to get started** — know where to begin
3. **Why you would do it** — the potential benefits of getting involved
4. **Why you might want to give it a miss** — not every tool suits every person
5. **Sharpening your presence** — plain English, practical tips for how to make the most of the time you spend, including recommendations for further reading and tools that can help